A TASTE OF PARADISE

A TASTE OF PARADISE

tastes & sights from paradise island

ariel reines

ISBN: 978-976-8108-87-6
Printed in Singapore

contents

introduction

I grew up perched on the end of a pier in the middle of Nassau Harbor. From the Dockhouse – our tiny, shingle-covered home precariously connected to Paradise Island by a one hundred-yard dock – I would watch life sail past. Over its forty years of existence, all manner of vehicles have passed by the Dockhouse: proud polished yachts, brave bobbing sailboats, colorful Haitian sloops, and rugged fishing boats, bellies heavy with the day's catch. These days we also watch cargo boats, speedboats, rowboats, sinking boats, and probably most of all ferryboats, affectionately named "Bum Boats," heave their load of curious visitors back and forth across the harbor.

We are not the only inquisitive ones. Just as we watch the tides of hustle and bustle wash in and out, we are constantly reminded that we too are being watched. While we sit out on our deck for lunch, a Bum Boat, half-drowning with passengers, chugs by the Dockhouse. The flashes of cameras and the points and waves inevitably begin while a tour guide delivers a charmingly fabricated story about our lives. I too have often traveled to and from Nassau on the Bum Boats, and always find myself peering curiously, as if from a stranger's eye, at our little house on the end of the dock.

It was thus that I began this book – an invitation to all of those boats and visitors who have sailed by to join me at the Dockhouse – to share the tastes, sights, and history of Paradise Island. The recipes in this book have been shared with family and friends and served often in this beautiful setting. Included are many traditional Bahamian recipes but also family dishes that I love and wished to share. To complement the recipes I have included a photographic tour of Paradise Island, as well as historical and cultural facts about the island. I thus invite you to join us, delve in, and discover for yourself a taste of paradise!

a history of paradise

For an in-depth review of the fascinating history of Paradise Island refer to *The Paradise Island Story* by Paul Albury. A beautiful, illustrated new edition was published in 2004.

Paradise Island did not begin as the tranquil, idyllic place that its name suggests. Its history is rife with unruly savages and brutal slavery, with thieves and corrupt politicians, and with shipwrecks and sunken gold. Paradise Island has seen a marvelous evolution from the days of pirates and treasure-hunters to the rising up of a new Atlantis.

The first settlers of the Bahamian Islands were the Lukku-cairi or Island People, also known as the Arawaks or Lucayans. These natives of South America made their way up through the Caribbean islands, arriving in the Bahamas during the ninth century A.D. They were a gentle, socially advanced people who lived in theocratic kingdoms, with a pantheon of gods whom they believed protected them from disease and disaster. Although they left no written record, artifacts, discovered by archeologists, map out their doomed existence.

Christopher Columbus landed on the Bahamian island of San Salvador in his historic voyage of 1492. His first landing in the "New World" brought the Bahamas into the consciousness of the Western world. The Spanish named the islands "Baja Mar," or "shallow waters"–a name that phonetically mimics the one we use today. The gentle indigenous population, estimated at 40,000 in 1492, was decimated within twenty-five years of the Spanish landing. Many suffered the ravages of foreign diseases to which they held no immunity, while those who were healthy were enslaved and shipped off to work in the mines of Hispaniola, the island now shared by Haiti and the Dominican Republic.

The first Bahamian Island to be settled was Eleuthera, then known as Cigatoo, in the mid 1640s by a group of English colonists who had previously settled in Bermuda. They set sail from Bermuda to escape puritanical religious persecution. Their ship met disaster in the shallow waters and ran aground en route. In a heroic effort, they made it to the shores of Eleuthra in small rowboats. They managed to send word to their base in Virginia to send supplies and thus established a thriving agricultural community and the first independent republic in the New World.

One of these colonists, Captain William Sayle, is thought to have been responsible for the discovery and first settlement of Nassau during a voyage headed for the Carolinas. During his journey, his ship was met by a ferocious storm and was set off course. Amidst bitter winds and tearing sails, he found his way into Nassau Harbor where he and his crew were able to wait out the storm, safe from the harm of the winds and raging sea. Feeling that he had been led to this haven of safety by a divine force, he named the island Providence (1). The name has changed little over the years, and the island is now known as New Providence.

During the sixteenth and seventeenth centuries the growth of the American colonies transformed the waters of the Bahamas into bustling shipping lanes. In return for supplies from Europe, galleons laden with treasure from the empires of Central and South America were sent back to Spain. The islands of the Bahamas provided shelter and supplies of wood, salt, and water to the passing vessels. The luxury of refueling in these shallow waters, however, came at a high price. The uncharted jagged reefs captured many a galleon in their sharp jaws, littering the seabed with sunken wrecks and drifting treasure.

Where treasure lay, pirates soon followed. Among the infamous pirates who dominated these waters was Blackbeard, born Edward Teach. He would weave hemp into his long beard and light it on fire before he attacked. His victims often surrendered before a shot was fired when they saw him standing on the deck wielding pistols and knifes, with his black beard flaming. He was notorious for marooning his own crew on desert islands if they displayed any sign of resistance.

Stories of buried gold and sunken galleons attracted treasure hunters from across the world. One of the most successful treasure hunts of all time was that of the New England-born shipbuilder William Phips. In 1641, an ill-fated Spanish silver fleet fell victim to a hurricane and lost its most valuable ship, the Concepción. The massive hull, filled to the brim with treasures of the Americas, ran aground and sank on the shallow reefs of the Bahamian waters. The five hundred-strong crew set about making rafts in a frenzy, and while two hundred men survived the storm, the Concepción and all of its treasure were lost to the hungry mouth of the seas.

In 1670, King Charles II claimed the largely uninhabited archipelago and named the first settlement on the north shore of New Providence Charles Town. Phips soon preyed on the king's gambling spirit to raise money for his treasure hunt. Intrigued by this romantic tale of treasure and the prospect of fortune, Charles II loaned Phips a Royal Navy ship to search for the Concepción some forty-two years after it had sunk. For months Phips swept the Bahamian waters without success, until his resources were depleted and his crew despondent. Phips returned to England to find that King Charles II had died and his successor wanted nothing to do with him.

Determined to resume his treasure hunt, Phips managed to find backing by the Duke of Albermale, who had already whittled away most of his family fortune through gambling and lavish living. On January 20, 1687, Phips and his men were scouring the waters in small crafts when, as luck would have it, one of his crew sighted a coral head deep in the water. Phips sent one of the divers out of his way to retrieve it for him as a keepsake. The diver not only brought back the coral, but also a gold coin from the sea floor. The Concepción had been found!

An eyewitness account recorded:

> And so the dollars they hoisted in by whole chests of 2,000 dollars together, for although the chests were rotted off and consumed, yet the dollars, with rust, were so grown together that they hung together as one lump—although the middle-most of the chest was bright and sound—and not many of them was much wasted by the water (2).

Phips returned to London with his ships laden with 37,538 pounds of pieces of eight, twenty-five pounds of gold, and 2,755 pounds of silver. One tenth of this treasure went to the king, one sixteenth to Phips, and the rest to his investors. He was knighted and appointed the first Royal Governor of Massachusetts.

Phips developed a great fondness for the port from which he made his fortune and had plans to settle there despite the absence of a rule of law. Indeed, during the seventeenth and beginning of the eighteenth centuries New Providence was governed by corrupt, incapable politicians. With inadequate defenses it fell prey to yearly pillages by the Spanish. Phips offered the Bahamian Grand Council a vast one thousand pounds to buy Paradise Island, then known simply as the "Island That Makes the Harbour," with the promise of matching that money in building defenses on New Providence. His offer, however, was refused and the land was kept for the common people. But in 1698, the island was sold, to the dismay of its inhabitants, for the small sum of fifty pounds to the former governor of New Providence, Nicholas Trott. He took the initiative to give his new purchase the rather unfortunate name of Hog Island, probably after the place where he was raised, Hog Bay, Bermuda. (3)

The Spanish continued with their terrifying attacks in which they would decimate the town and kill all inhabitants who could not find safe hiding amidst the caves and woods. As the story goes, the Spanish roasted one governor, Robert Clark, on a spit! With indefatigable tenacity, however, Charles Town would rise again after each attack, until the total collapse of government after a particularly brutal onslaught in 1704. The pirates took control of the capital and created a "Privateers' Republic" without government or laws, appointing Blackbeard as their chief and magistrate. The pirates did a roaring business, looting passing galleons and using the caves and cays of the Bahamian Islands as hideouts for their loot. Rumors of buried treasure persist today. Pirate William Cat allegedly hid his vast riches in a secret spot on Cat Island, while Henry Morgan is said to have buried his treasure on Andros Island.

The industry of privateering began to boom in the Bahamas. Privateering was essentially a government-sanctioned form of piracy that allowed private vessels to act as war vessels, capture enemy ships, and pillage their contents. This was only supposed to be permitted during war, but indeed the rules of privateering were easily and often transgressed into common pirating. Privateers prospered in Nassau, where raids were easily made and the loot could be obtained without government interference. Such privateers plundered French and Spanish ships during the War of Spanish Succession. When peace was declared in 1714, the privateers continued to make their living illegally. At this time there were over one thousand pirates making their living off the Bahamian waters. Having seen a multitude of corrupt governors, Nassau was essentially a wasteland of ruined forts and ungoverned people.

At this point, the British authorities stepped in to restore order to Nassau and appointed the first royal governor, Woodes Rogers. Rogers, too, had made his livelihood as a successful privateer. In 1709, during a voyage around the world, he not only intercepted and seized a Spanish galleon laden with riches, he also found a castaway marooned on a desert island named Alexander Selkirk who later became the inspiration for Daniel Defoe's character–Robinson Crusoe!

junkanoo

The celebration of the Junkanoo, a combination of dance and music with roots in Western Africa, probably dates back to the sixteenth or seventeenth century. Around Christmas, Bahamian slaves were given a few days off. This allowed them to leave the plantations to be with their families and to celebrate the holiday with music, dance, and costumes. Various theories have been advanced regarding the etymology of the word "Junkanoo." Some believe the name is from the French "gens inconnus," which means "the unknown people" and could allude to the fact that the participants are masked and disguised and therefore "unknown." The most popular belief is that the word is derived from "John Canoe," an African tribal chief who demanded he be allowed the right to celebrate with his people even after he was brought to the West Indies as a slave.

Woodes Rogers first stepped foot on Nassau on 27 July, 1718, landing at Fort Nassau, which now holds the foundations of the Sheraton-British Colonial Hotel. He was greeted by a parade of pirates who lined up to assess their new governor. Rogers bore down on them with a firm hand right then and there. He pardoned all past crimes but banned any future pirating under penalty of death. Indeed, over the coming year, the corpses of men who broke his law would often be seen swaying from the gallows set up next to the harbor to warn future offenders. Such tactics proved effective, and Rogers managed to put an end to pirating and to rebuild Nassau's defenses. Rogers also managed to rid the islands of the threat of Blackbeard, who had moved elsewhere in the Caribbean to escape the fate of the other pirates. In 1718 a British ship sought him out and fought a bloody battle in which Blackbeard received "five pistol balls and twenty cutlass wounds" before he finally died. The Royal Navy captain then decapitated Blackbeard and flaunted his success by hanging Blackbeard's head on the ship's rigging.

In 1776 the American Revolutionary War was declared, and in 1782 the Spanish, who entered on the side of the Americans, seized the Bahamas. Hog Island was thick with dense forest and served as a hideout for many of the inhabitants of Nassau, who would lumber their possessions across the channel and seek refuge from attacking forces. A year later, under the Treaty of Versailles, Hog Island once again became a British colony, and thousands of English Loyalists came to live under British reign in the Bahamas. They brought with them their slaves and building and agricultural skills and attempted to replant their cotton plantations. When slavery was outlawed in 1807, the Bahamas became a drop-off point for freed slaves. The Royal Navy would intercept slave ships and deposit the slaves on the islands of the Bahamas while carting their captains off to court. In the early 1800s, many of the Loyalists moved away from the Bahamas in search of more fertile soil and left their land to their freed slaves.

The 826 acres of Hog Island were divided up at this point into a number of different lots. The two largest lots (240 and 300 acres, respectively) went to the governor of the Bahamas, Lord Dunmore, and to the Florida ship builder John Russell. Substantially smaller lots were divided between Sarah Carmichael, the war department, and the Crown Land. Cannon batteries and a small hospital were built to defend the strategically located island. The hospital acted as a quarantine station during outbreaks of yellow fever, typhoid, smallpox, and cholera. Later on, tiny Athol Island, on the eastern tip of Hog Island, was converted into a fully equipped isolation and quarantine unit for ill residents and for incoming crews.

The Bahamas thrived off the troubled times of the neighboring mainland. In 1861, during the American Civil War, the Union Navy blockaded the Islands in an attempt to cripple the Confederacy. Bahamians grew rich running confederate cotton to English mills in return for military equipment on large vessels named Blockade-Runners. John Russell took advantage of the superior timber in the Bahamas and the need to make frequent repairs on the Blockade-Runners and opened a large shipyard on Hog Island. The shipyard business boomed. The marine railways just to the west of the Dockhouse can be seen from the air today. Hog Island also played host to the largest coaling station of the Bahamas storing up to 50,000 tons of coal that fueled the Blockade-Runners.

Peace was declared in 1865, and again New Providence plunged into hard times. To add insult to injury, a vast fire broke out at the Hog Island dockyards that were storing two thousand cases of petroleum salvaged from a wreck in Grand Bahama. Two fire engines sped to the harbor shore where, across the channel, Hog Island was rapidly losing its battle to the raging flames. It was decided to bring one engine over on a raft and the other on a barge. To the dismay of the on-looking residents and townspeople, the raft capsized under the enormous weight of the engine. The barge made it across and was able to finally contain the fire, but only after the entire dockyard had been consumed. When the shipyard was rebuilt, a vast modern marine railway and dry dock were installed.

A bulk storage facility for oil arose next door to the Nassau Boat Works, owned by the West India Oil Company, that would later be known as Esso. The sturdy Esso dock that played host to the oil tankers was the perfect foundation for the Dockhouse that Sam Clapp built in 1965.

Tourism began to sprout its early roots in the 1890s. Vacations under the sun became a popular pursuit, and Americans started to branch out and explore the relatively unchartered Bahamian beaches. A number of "bathing houses" arose on the long white beach of Hog Island to take advantage of society's newfound love of swimming. Previously this had been considered a dirty and unhealthy pursuit. For twenty-four cents, a visitor could take a ferry to Hog Island and spend the day at a bathing house that not only provided changing rooms and fresh fruits, but also bathing suits! Much to the chagrin of the more conservative bathers, one of the bathing houses appeared to have a perpetual shortage of bathing suits so its visitors took to bathing nude.

In 1897 J L Saunders took the bathing houses to a new level and developed a resort named "Casino." Activities not only included swimming, dining, and dancing but also bowling, billiards, and fireworks. To attract visitors, he organized spectacles such as trapeze artists, tightrope walkers, dancing lessons, theatre performances, bicycle and sack races, and lavish feasts.

In the early 1900s tourism began to take a firm hold. This was largely pioneered by American Frank Munson, who built Nassau's first two hotels. He also ran the Munson Steamship Line that was comprised of three ships accommodating over 250 passengers each that traveled between New York and Nassau. Hog Island soon became a playground for America's wealthiest heirs and heiresses, who set up their winter homes there. The Porcupine Club, one of the world's most exclusive social clubs, was opened on the island in 1913. With only fifty members at its largest capacity, the multi-millionaires, including J.P. Morgan, Andrew Mellon, Howard Hughes, and Vincent Astor, would dock their magnificent yachts at the yellow harborside building. Unfortunately, the Porcupine Club became a victim of its own exclusivity: it was so reluctant to let new members in that eventually the existing members died out and the club dissolved. In an ironic twist of fate, the site of the Porcupine Club was later transformed into the restaurant of the "all-inclusive" Club Med resort.

Prohibition during the "Roaring Twenties" transformed the Bahamas into a base for rum-running, and Nassau's waterfront soon grew into a vast rum warehouse. Profits from this illicit business were poured into the construction of hotels and the building of the first casino and the island flourished into a popular vacation spot for America's rich and famous, who were lured by the crystal waters, gambling opportunities, and easy access to liquor.

In 1928, Munson persuaded the Bahamian government to dredge and deepen the harbor to allow his steamships to dock in Nassau rather than out at sea with ferry services. The government agreed and built Prince George Wharf, which has since been expanded multiple times to accommodate the ever-growing cruise line industry. However, the repeal of prohibition in 1933 sent the Bahamas back into an economic slump that worsened during the Great Depression and the government's attempts to subsidize Munson's steamship and hotel business were unsuccessful. He soon went bankrupt and not long after met an early end in an automobile accident. The overall slump lasted until the 1940s when, during World War II, the Bahamas served as an air and sea way station bringing a wave of GIs followed by a boom in tourism.

A Swedish industrialist, Dr. Wenner-Gren, bought a magnificent site on the Eastern tip of the island in 1939 from the Lynch estate (of the brokerage house Merrill, Lynch, and Co.) Wenner-Gren paid $150,000 for it and proceeded to build his "Shangri-La," which is Tibetan for "land of sacredness and peace." Some twenty years later, in 1960, he sold it to Huntington Hartford II, the wealthy heir to A&P supermarkets for $13 million. The deal is said to have been signed on the back of a menu card during a dinner at Shangri-La. It was Hartford and Wenner-Gren who had the idea of finding a more alluring name for Hog Island. On May 23, 1962 an act of legislature decreed the following: "From and after the coming into force of this Act the island lying to the North of the island of New Providence heretofore known as Hog island shall be called and referred to as Paradise island."

the cloisters

The fourteenth Century Augustine cloister now on the property of the Ocean Club was purchased in France by the American newspaper giant William Randolph Hearst. It was subsequently bought by Huntington Hartford, the A&P supermarket heir and developer of Paradise Island, and flown to Nassau in pieces. Much to the dismay of the expert in stone recreation that he employed, the pieces arrived with no instruction at all in how to reassemble the cloister–thus the operation took over a year.

Hartford proceeded to set in motion the events that would make Paradise Island a world-renowned destination. He built a fifty-two-room hotel named the Ocean Club on the site of Shangri-La, he built the Hurricane Hole Marina that could hold sixty-five yachts, and he built a golf course on the Eastern end of the island. In accomplishing this great vision, Hartford would plunder his fortune and spend the rest of his life destitute in New York's Bronx.

Soon, Paradise Island became a safe haven for a diverse group including rock stars, actors, artists, and social icons. Indeed, while strolling along Paradise Beach in the late 1960s, one might have come across Eric Clapton and Ronnie Woods strumming their guitars in the sand, smelled the exotic aromas from George Harrison's Indian-inspired cooking, or stumbled upon Timothy Leary, the Harvard Psychology Professor who lost his tenure after urging students to use LSD and "turn on, tune in, and drop out."

While the country was gaining a permanent foothold in international tourism with the closure of nearby Cuba and the arrival of the jet age, it was also turning a corner in its history. Great Britain granted the islands self-government in 1964 and changed their status from colony to commonwealth in 1969. The Commonwealth of Bahamas became an independent nation on July 10, 1973, which is celebrated today as Bahamian Independence Day. The nation's independence rekindled the gambling tourism as well as the islands' status as a tax haven. By the 1970s, Paradise Island saw a renewed boom in tourism, thanks in large part to the development of gaming resorts.

Club Med opened its doors on the estate of the Porcupine Club on December 10, 1977. To the west of this land lies the yoga retreat, a quiet village with small cabins that house vacationers who prefer to meditate and pursue the discipline of yoga. This land was given to the Swami Vishnu Devenanda by the daughter of H.C. Albury as a ninety-nine-year lease in return for his spiritual guidance. A myriad of hotels sprang up on the island throughout the 1980s, as Paradise Island became an ever-more popular vacation spot.

The boom in the tourism industry culminated in the development of one of the world's most spectacular resorts, Atlantis. Kerzner International started purchasing land and facilities in 1993 and now owns over seventy percent of the island. The spectacular development currently features three interconnected hotel towers, a seven-acre lagoon, and a thirty-four-acre marine environment. Further expansion is already in the plans and an additional 1,500 rooms will be added over the next several years. What is already the largest man-made open marine habitat in the world with eleven million gallons of water, two hundred sea species and fifty thousand animals, will grow to include additional water-theme parks and a dolphin encounter. The casino, the largest in the Caribbean with nine hundred slot machines and seventy-eight gaming tables, will no doubt continue to attract its share of visitors, the luckiest of whom might elect to enjoy their stay perched in the breathtaking suite connecting the Royal Towers, far removed from the tales of savages, shipwrecks, and pirates.

References:
1. Mary Moseley, The Bahamas Handbook, (Nassau, 1926)
2. Arthur C. Clarke, The Treasure of the Great Reef (Scholastic, 1964)
3. Paul Albury, The Story of the Bahamas (Macmillan, 1984, 2004)

in the beginning

bahamian conch fritters

chilled cucumber soup

avocado gazpacho soup

steaming souffléd artichoke dip

baked garlic brie

melted crab dip

chunky guacamole

bahamian conch chowder

bahamian conch fritters with spicy dipping sauce

Conch fritters are a delightful start to an authentic Bahamian evening. They are a staple of almost any Bahamian party and can be made easily in large batches.

Fritters:
2 conchs, pounded, cleaned, and diced

1/2 tomato, diced

1/2 green pepper, diced

1/2 large onion, diced

1 cup milk

1 1/2 cups flour

1 egg

1 tsp baking powder

1 tsp salt

1 tsp hot sauce

1 Tbsp fresh lime juice

Sauce:
1 cup mayonnaise

1/2 cup ketchup

1 Tbsp horseradish

1 tsp hot sauce

1 Stir together the fritter ingredients using a fork.

2 Let the batter sit for 30 minutes and stir. Add more milk or flour as needed to make a thick batter consistency.

3 Heat a deep fryer or pot of oil until it is almost smoking.

4 Drop the batter, one tablespoon at a time, into the hot oil and cook until the fritters are puffed and golden brown.

5 Mix together the ingredients for the sauce until blended. Serve the fritters in baskets with toothpicks, a sprinkle of fresh lime juice, and the sauce on the side.

Serves 4-6

caribbean conchs

The Queen Conch, or Strombus Gigas, can be found from Brazil through the West Indies, Florida, and Bermuda. They have, however, been vastly depleted by over fishing and now exist in large numbers only in the Bahamas. Here they are a traditional food staple and a national symbol. An estimated 500 000 lbs of conch are consumed in the Bahamas each year!

chilled cucumber soup with fresh herb garnish

This is the perfect soup for a hot summer's evening - it is remarkably refreshing and satisfying. It has been a favorite at the Dockhouse for many years.

3 large English cucumbers, peeled and sliced

2 large yellow onions

2 oz. butter

1 tsp sugar

1 egg yolk

1/2 cup heavy cream

2 cups chicken broth

Dill, parsley, chives

Sour cream for garnish

ice serving bowl

Half-fill a large Pyrex bowl with water. Place a second, smaller bowl inside and tape the bowl down so that the water forms a bowl. Freeze the water bowl overnight. Briefly dip in warm water to unmold.

1 In a large, deep cooking pot fry the onions in the butter over a medium-low heat until the onions are very soft but NOT brown.

2 Add the sugar and 2 of the peeled and sliced cucumbers. Stir for 1 minute.

3 Add 2 cups of chicken broth and simmer over a low heat for 30 minutes.

4 Allow to cool for 20 minutes and then puree the soup in a blender.

5 Transfer the soup to a large bowl. Beat the egg yolk and the cream together using a whisk, then whisk into the soup.

6 Refrigerate until cold - preferably overnight.

7 A few hours before serving add a handful of fresh herbs and 1 peeled and sliced cucumber to 1 cup of the prepared soup and beat the mixture in a blender. Stir this mixture into the rest of the soup.

8 Chill the soup bowls in the freezer before serving.

9 Ladle the soup into the cold bowls and garnish with sour cream and chopped fresh herbs.

Serves 4

avocado gazpacho soup with vegetable crudités

I like to serve this soup with small bowls full of chopped onions, tomatoes, peppers and cucumbers. The vegetables add flavor and texture the soup and are great healthy alternatives to croutons.

1 large cucumber, peeled

1 large ripe avocado

1 green bell pepper

1 red bell pepper

1/4 cup celery

1/4 cup green onions

1/4 cup white wine

1/4 cup olive oil

1 Tbsp red wine vinegar

2 cups beef broth

4 cups tomatoes, chopped

2 tsp sugar

1 Tbsp cilantro

1 Mix all of the ingredients in a mixer and puree. You may need to do this in batches, depending on the size of the mixer being used.

2 Refrigerate the pureed soup overnight.

3 Serve the soup in chilled bowls with garnishes of chopped onion, peppers, cucumbers, and tomatoes.

Serves 4-6

bahamian geography

The Bahamas are made up of seven hundred islands that lie in the Atlantic Ocean. The islands are low-lying and made up of coral and limestone. Indeed, the Bahamas hold about five percent of the world's coral in their turquoise waters. The subtropical climate cultivates a host of wild plants and animals including bougainvillaea, hibiscus, oleander, iguanas, boa constrictors, flamingos, parrots, and humming birds.

steaming souffléd artichoke dip with parmesan

This is one of my most popular dishes at any party, be it casual evening drinks or a formal dinner. It is surprisingly simple to prepare and absolutely delicious. I have actually made this recipe without the artichokes and it is still great.

1 8oz can artichoke hearts drained and chopped into small pieces

1/2 onion, finely chopped

1 cup mayonnaise (full fat!)

1 cup parmesan cheese

1 tsp Worcester sauce

1 tsp Tabasco

1 egg (optional)

1 Preheat the oven to 350° and combine all of the ingredients in a Pyrex bowl or another small dish suitable for serving. For a creamier dip do not add the egg; for a more souffléd version add a beaten egg to the mixture.

2 Bake at 375° for 40 minutes or until the mixture is browned and puffed.

3 This is delicious served straight out of the hot bowl with watercrackers or tortilla chips.

Serves 6-8
40 minutes
375°

elegant parmesan rounds

If you want a less rustic and more elegant effect, you can cut 2-inch rounds of bread and place them on a baking sheet. Spoon the uncooked mixture onto the bread and bake at 350° for 10 - 15 minutes until golden brown.

baked garlic brie in a golden pastry crust

This is so easy and always looks spectacular. You can prepare it a day ahead and bake it just before you plan to serve it.

1 pie crust pastry

1 round brie cheese

3 cloves garlic, chopped

1 egg yolk, lightly whisked

1 Place the brie in the center of the rolled-out pie pastry, sprinkle the top with the garlic, and fold the pastry around the cheese so it is completely covered and sealed.

2 Trim the extra pastry and decorate as desired with pastry leaves.

3 Brush the pastry with the egg yolk and bake at 375° for 45 minutes, covering with foil if the pastry browns too much.

Serves 6-8
45 minutes
375°

decorative pastry leaves

Pastry leaves add a sophisticated touch to this dish. Simply cut a leaf-shaped piece from the extra pastry. Use a sharp knife to score a line in the middle, along the length of the pastry leaf. Then make diagonal lines from the center line to the edge of the leaf. Place the leaves decoratively on top of the covered brie, gluing with a little water on the underside, before baking.

melted crab dip with garlic and green onions

Crabs are abundant in Nassau and are found in many typical Bahamian dishes. They are often stewed and served with peas and rice for a hearty breakfast! This dip is one of my favorite ways to enjoy fresh crab meat but can also be made with canned crab.

6 oz fresh crab meat

8 oz cream cheese

3 Tbsp white wine

1 clove garlic, minced

3 chopped green onions

2 Tbsp mayonnaise

1 tsp Worcester sauce

1 tsp Tabasco

1/4 cup parmesan cheese

1 Mix all of the ingredients together in a Pyrex bowl except for the cheese.

2 Sprinkle the parmesan cheese on top.

3 Bake at 350° for 30 minutes or until golden.

4 Serve with chips or crackers.

Serves 4-6
30 minutes
350°

bahamian crabs

The island of Andros has the largest population of land crabs in the Bahamas and celebrates an annual Andros Crabfest. This occurs in June when the crabs take to the road on their journey from their burrows to the sea where they lay their eggs. This annual spectacle of hundreds of thousands of crabs trekking to the ocean begins three nights before the full moon.

chunky guacamole with sweet tomato and cilantro

Avocados are easy to find in Nassau. If possible use Hass avocados since these have the creamiest texture. If using Bahamian avocados add an extra tablespoon of olive oil to the recipe.

3 Hass avocados

1 ripe tomato, diced

1/2 yellow onion, finely chopped

1 Tbsp cilantro, chopped

2 Tbsp olive oil

1 tsp Tabasco

1 tsp sugar

1 tsp salt

Pepper

1   Mash the avocados into a chunky paste with a fork.

2   Add the rest of the ingredients and mix.

3   Add salt and pepper to taste and transfer to a serving bowl.

4   Serve with crackers or tortilla chips.

Serves 2-4

cook's tip

Leave an avocado pit in the guacamole until serving. This will keep the guacamole from discoloring if it is made ahead of time.

bahamian conch chowder with tomatoes & thyme

Bahamian conch chowder is red and lacks the cream base of its New England counterpart, clam chowder. The flavors of the thyme, tomatoes, and conch blend beautifully to make this delicious soup. It can be served with crusty bread for lunch or as a starter for dinner.

2 conchs, cleaned and bruised

4 strips bacon, chopped

1 onion, finely chopped

1 green pepper, finely chopped

1/2 small hot pepper, finely chopped

4 large tomatoes, finely chopped

1 Tbsp tomato paste

1 bay leaf

6 fresh thyme branches

1 tsp salt

2 cups chicken broth

2 Tbsp heavy cream

1 Bring a quart of salted water to a rapid boil and add the conch. Boil for 3 minutes.

2 Remove the conch, drain, and finely chop, using scissors.

3 Fry the bacon in a large skillet until it is golden. Add the onion and fry over a medium heat for 5 minutes.

4 Add the green pepper and hot pepper and fry for 5 minutes. Add the tomatoes, tomato paste, salt, bay leaf, and the fresh thyme and simmer, partially covered, over a low heat for 10 minutes.

5 Add the chicken broth and simmer for 40 minutes, adding more broth if it becomes too reduced. Add the conch during the last 10 minutes of cooking.

6 Remove the chowder from the heat and stir in the cream.

Serves 4
60 minutes

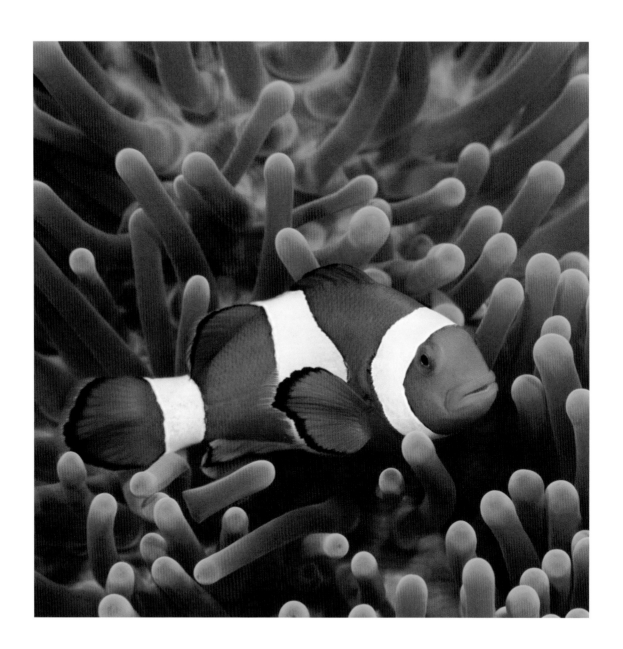

salads

brilliant bean salad

mozzarella & tomato salad

grilled goat cheese salad

pear & gorgonzola salad

tangy mustard vinaigrette

brilliant bean salad with curry and turmeric

This is an incredibly easy and versatile salad. Any combination of beans works well. I add tuna for a more substantial dish. This salad is far more elegant and delicious than the ingredients suggest!

1 can lima beans, rinsed

1 can navy beans, rinsed

1 can kidney beans, rinsed

1 can chick peas, rinsed

1 can corn, rinsed

1 large tomato, diced

1 yellow onion, diced

1 cucumber, seeded and diced

1 can tuna (if desired)

2 tsp curry powder

1 tsp turmeric

8 Tbsp "tangy mustard vinaigrette" (see end of chapter)

Salt

Pepper

1 Mix all of the ingredients together in a large bowl.

2 Sprinkle with extra olive oil if dry and serve in small bowls or on a bed of lettuce with warm bread.

Serves 6

the ocean club

The Ocean Club, located on the east end of Paradise Island, is one of the most beautiful and exclusive resorts in the Caribbean. The perfectly kept, lush grounds are full of quiet spots for enjoying a view and forgetting the outside world. The site of the Ocean Club has long served as a luxurious retreat. It was owned in the 1930s by Edmund Lynch of Merrill, Lynch & Co. and then purchased in 1939 by industrialist - Dr. Wenner-Gren. He named his property Shangri-La after the Tibetan utopian monastery. It was Wenner-Gren who began the construction of the exquisite gardens that can now be visited on the southern aspect of the Ocean Club. These gardens are terraced into seven levels and extend upwards towards the cloisters that overlook the harbor. The gardens are filled with flowers, statues ,and fountains and continue to be perfectly kept sixty years after their conception.

mozzarella & tomato salad with fragrant basil

This is a Dockhouse staple. The key to its success is to use only the best tomatoes and mozzarella for this salad. Basil thrives in Nassau's salty humidity at all times of the year.

1 cup fresh buffalo mozzarella

4 vine ripe tomatoes

1 bunch fresh basil

Extra-virgin olive oil

Balsamic vinegar

Salt

Fresh ground pepper

1 Slice the mozzarella and tomato and shred the basil.

2 Layer these three ingredients alternately. Sprinkle each layer with the salt and pepper.

3 Drizzle olive oil and balsamic vinegar over the salad in proportions of about 3:1 and let sit for 10 minutes for juices to flow.

4 Delicious served with warm bread and sliced avocado.

Serves 2-4

the little red house

The little red house is a typical example of the charming and colorful Bahamian architecture seen throughout the islands. The houses are usually wooden and brightly colored in pastel pinks, yellows, and greens. Bahamian architecture was greatly influenced by the British Loyalists who fled the newly formed United States in the 1700s.

grilled goat cheese salad with toasted croutons

This is a perfect starter for almost any dinner. It is easy, delicious, and always looks wonderful. You can also make a few extra cheese croutons and serve it as a light main course.

8 oz goat cheese

1 baguette

1/2 cup "tangy mustard vinaigrette" (see end of chapter)

Mixed salad greens

1/2 package cherry tomatoes

1 cucumber, seeded and chopped

1 bunch chives, chopped

Salt

Freshly ground pepper

1 Cut the baguette crossways into 8 1/2-inch thick slices.

2 Cut 8 1-inch thick rounds of the goat cheese and place one on each bread slice.

3 Sprinkle the cheese and bread with salt and freshly ground pepper and then cover any protruding bread edges with foil so they do not burn under the broiler.

4 Place the cheese croutons on a baking tray, drizzle with some of the vinaigrette, and broil for 5-10 minutes or until the cheese is golden brown. (Watch out for burning!)

5 Mix together the greens, tomatoes, cucumber and chives with the rest of the salad dressing and serve on 4 individual plates.

6 Divide the warm croutons equally among the 4 plates. Place them on top of the salad and sprinkle with salt, pepper, and a little olive oil.

Serves 4

gorgonzola salad with roasted pear & candy pecans

This is one of my favorite salads because it has such a wonderful combination of flavors and textures. The sweet crunch of the pecans complements the strong cheese perfectly. It is delicious served with steak or lamb.

6 oz gorgonzola, crumbled

1 small package cherry tomatoes, halved

Mixed salad greens

2 Bosc pears, sliced

1 cup pecans

1/2 cup sugar

2 Tbsps vegetable oil

1/2 cup "tangy mustard vinaigrette"

Freshly ground pepper

1 Place the oil and sugar in a heavy skillet and heat over a medium heat until the sugar is melted and golden brown.

2 Add the pears and the pecans and stir over a medium heat for 3 minutes. Be careful not to let the pecans burn.

3 Remove the pear and pecan mixture from the heat and pour into a foil-lined tray. Let the mixture cool and harden. Separate any pecans that are stuck together.

4 Mix together the salad greens, tomatoes, cheese, pecans, pears, and dressing.

5 Serve with plenty of cracked pepper and mustard vinaigrette.

Serves 4

tangy mustard vinaigrette with cracked pepper

I use this vinaigrette on almost every salad I make. The trick is the sugar that balances the spiciness of the mustard and the tang of the vinegar. If the dressing is too tangy, add a little more sugar and a little more olive oil. I use either red, white, or balsamic vinegar depending on my mood - all are delicious.

1 cup extra-virgin olive oil

1/4 cup vinegar

1/3 cup Dijon mustard

3 Tbsp sugar

2 tsp salt

1 Tbsp cracked pepper

1 Tbsp water

1 Place all of the ingredients together in a large jar.

2 Shake the jar with the lid on until all of the ingredients are well mixed and the dressing is thick and creamy.

Makes 2 cups dressing

properties in paradise

This yellow house, a typical example of colonial Bahamian style, was built by the Irish filmographer, screenwriter and producer Kevin McClory, who produced the James Bond films *Thunderball* and *Never Say Never Again*. The large wooden house on the prior page was constructed for the set of one of his movies, then dismantled and shipped to Paradise Island, where McClory had the house reassembled on his property.

from the sea

grilled grouper

traditional steam conch

bahamian conch salad

roasted salmon fillets

fresh tuna carpaccio

grilled grouper with soy-ginger glaze & coconut

In Nassau we use grouper, the Bahamian member of the Sea Bass family, for this dish, but salmon can be substituted for the grouper and it tastes even better! This is delicious served on a bed of mashed potatoes mixed with a tablespoon of wasabi or horseradish sauce and a side of steamed bok choy.

5 Tbsps soy sauce

1 Tbsp fresh ginger, grated

1 Tbsp Worcester sauce

3 Tbsps honey

1 Tsp rice wine vinegar

3 Tbsps water

2 tsp cornstarch mixed with equal parts of water

3 Tbsps chilled butter

1/2 cup coconut milk

Salt and pepper

4-6 fillets sea bass

1 Mix the soy sauce, honey, rice vinegar, Worcester sauce, ginger, and water in a small saucepan and stir over a medium-low heat.

2 Add the cornstarch and water mixture and stir over the heat until the glaze boils and thickens slightly.

3 Remove from the heat, allow to cool slightly, then add the chilled butter, 1 tablespoon at a time, stirring constantly.

4 Cool the mixture and then store for up to 2 days in the refrigerator.

5 Warm the glaze slightly and spoon about half over the grouper fillets, reserving some for the sauce. Grill the fillets for about 5 minutes or until the fish is just cooked through.

6 Mix the remaining warm glaze with the coconut milk and drizzle around the grilled fish.

Serves 4

traditional steam conch with spicy peppers & thyme

This is one of my favorite Bahamian specialties. It brings out the unique texture and flavor of the conch and is often served with peas and rice or coleslaw. According to the ministry of tourism, steam conch is the nation's official "favorite dish".

2 conchs, cleaned and bruised

4 strips bacon, chopped

1 onion, chopped

1 green pepper, chopped

1/2 small hot pepper, chopped

4 large tomatoes, diced

1 Tbsp tomato paste

1 bay leaf

6 fresh thyme branches

1 cup water

1 tsp salt

1 Bring a quart of salted water to a rapid boil and add the conch.

2 Boil for 3 minutes and then remove the conch, drain, and roughly chop using scissors.

3 Fry the bacon in a large skillet until it is golden.

4 Add the onion and fry over a medium heat for 5 minutes, then add the green pepper and hot pepper and fry for 5 minutes.

5 Add the tomatoes, tomato paste, salt, bay leaf, and the fresh thyme and cook over a medium heat for 2 minutes.

6 Add the water and simmer, partially covered, over a low heat for 25 minutes.

7 Add the conch and simmer for a further 10 minutes, adding more water as necessary.

8 Serve with peas and rice and coleslaw for a truly Bahamian dinner!

Serves 4
50 minutes

bahamian conch salad with hot peppers and lime

Conch salad is a true Bahamian delicacy and it is worth a trip to Potter's Cay under the Paradise Island Bridge to watch the Bahamians make this salad to order. Be sure to make it fresh just before serving.

2 conchs, cleaned, scored and diced

1 small onion, diced

1 green pepper, diced

1 large tomato, diced

1/2 small hot pepper, seeded and chopped

1/2 cup fresh sour orange juice (can use lime to substitute)

2 Tbsps fresh lime juice

1 tsp coarse sea salt

1 Combine all of the ingredients in a large bowl, adding more salt if desired to taste.

2 Serve in glass bowls for a starter or light lunch.

Serves 2-4

a culinary tradition

Conch salad is one of the most traditional and delicious Bahamian specialties. It is always made fresh to order and the preparer of the conch salad is usually at the epicenter of a large social and jovial crowd. A trip to the conch salad stalls at Potter's Cay, under the eastern bridge crossing to Paradise Island, is not only a fascinating spectacle, but provides a delicious and inexpensive meal! Don't forget to try the conch fritters while you are there...

roasted salmon fillets over julienned vegetables

This is a wonderful dish for small dinner parties. It is elegant and absolutely delicious.

4-6 salmon fillets with bones and skin removed

1/3 cup white wine

1/2 lb salted butter

2 tsp fresh tarragon

1/3 cup light chicken broth

2 cups chopped leeks

1 cup julienned carrots

1 cup mushrooms, chopped

1 cup julienned zucchini

1 Preheat the oven to 350°.

2 Melt all but 2 tablespoons of the salted butter in a frying pan over a medium-low heat and sauté the vegetables for 5 minutes.

3 Place the salmon fillets in a baking dish surrounded and partly covered by the vegetable mixture. Dot the salmon with pats of the remaining butter and sprinkle the white wine and broth over the top. Top with salt and fresh tarragon.

4 Cover the dish tightly with foil and bake at 350° for 20 minutes or until the salmon is just cooked through.

5 Place the vegetables in the center of each plate and top with a fillet of salmon. Salt to taste.

Serves 4
350°
20 minutes

tuna carpaccio with dill-infused olive oil

Use only the freshest tuna for this dish and it will be delicious. When we are lucky enough to catch tuna on fishing trips, this is always the first dish I make. I prefer to serve it cold, with warm bread on the side to dip in the juices.

1 lb fresh tuna

1/2 onion, finely sliced

2 Tbsps capers

5 Tbsps olive oil

1/4 cup fresh Dill

Cracked pepper

Salt

1 Using a sharp knife, slice the tuna into very thin slices.

2 Arrange on a plate and sprinkle with the sliced onion.

3 Chop the dill and stir into the olive oil.

4 Pour the olive oil over the fresh tuna slices.

5 Sprinkle with salt, pepper, and capers if desired.

6 Serve at room temperature or chilled, with toasted baguette for dipping.

Serves 2-4

fishing in the bahamas

The Bahamas is one of the leading recreational deep-sea-fishing spots in the world and is the location for many an angling tournament. Fishing boats can be rented by the day, and the experienced captain will take you to all of the favored locations for catching tuna, mahi-mahi, and marlin.

from the land

chocolate chili

peanut drumsticks

barbeque sauce

mom's chicken soup

roasted garlic lamb

chocolate chili with melted cheddar & sour cream

1 onion, chopped

1 green pepper, chopped

3 Tbsps olive oil

4 cloves garlic, chopped

2 lbs lean ground beef

3 Tbsps chili powder

1 28-oz can chopped tomatoes

1 cup beef broth

1 bay leaf

1 tsp cayenne pepper

1 tsp Tabasco sauce

2 tsp dried oregano

2 tsp cinnamon

2 oz semi-sweet chocolate

2 Tbsp sugar

Chopped cilantro, onions, and peppers

Cheddar cheese and sour cream for garnish.

Salt and pepper to taste

1 In a large pot cook the onion, garlic, and green pepper in the olive oil, over a medium heat, until soft but not brown.

2 In a skillet, brown the beef, drain it well, and add it to the onion and peppers.

3 Add the chili powder and cook over a medium heat for 1 minute.

4 Add the tomatoes, broth, bay leaf, cayenne pepper, Tabasco, oregano, salt, and pepper.

5 Bring the mixture to a boil, reduce to a low heat, and simmer, partially covered, for 2 hours. Stir occasionally, adding water as necessary, to prevent burning.

6 Add the chocolate, sugar, and cinnamon and adjust the seasonings to taste.

7 Garnish with grated cheese, sour cream, diced peppers, onions, and cilantro.

chocolate

Christopher Columbus, who first discovered the Bahamas in 1492 on his voyage to the Americas, is said to have brought back cacao beans to King Ferdinand from his fourth visit to the New World, but they were overlooked in favor of the many other treasures he had found. Indeed, chocolate is an ingredient used for a great diversity of dishes in the Caribbean and South America and is often used to complement meats and poultry. In this dish it adds a wonderful depth of flavor to the chili without leaving it too sweet.

peanut drumsticks with spicy dipping sauce

This is an ideal dish for a beach picnic or boat outing. The drumsticks are delicious served hot or cold.

12 skinless chicken drum-sticks

5 Tbsps olive oil

2 tsp lemon juice

4 oz flour

2 Tbsps curry powder

1 tsp paprika

1 cup salted peanuts

2 Tbsps cilantro, finely chopped

2 eggs beaten

4 Tbsps milk

Pinch cayenne pepper

Sauce:

1/2 cup mayonnaise

1/2 cup sour cream

1 tsp sweet paprika

1 tsp cayenne pepper

1   Lay the drumsticks in a dish. Mix 2 tablespoons olive oil with the lemon juice and pour over the chicken. Leave the chicken to marinate overnight.

2   Mix the flour, curry, and paprika in a Ziplock bag. In a food processor, grind the nuts together with 2 tablespoons of the flour mixture, the cilantro, and the cayenne pepper.

3   Lightly beat the eggs with the milk in a bowl. Add the drumsticks to the Ziplock bag and toss in the flour mixture until the drumsticks are completely coated.

4   Next dip the drumsticks in the egg mixture, followed by the nut mix to coat the chicken. Refrigerate for up to 1 day until needed.

5   Heat the olive oil in a heavy baking tray at 425°, add the drumsticks, and bake on the high shelf of the oven, basting well, for 15 minutes.

6   Carefully turn the drumsticks and cook for another 8 minutes. Pour off the oil and cook the drumsticks for 5 more minutes or until very crisp.

7   Drain on a paper towel, mix together the ingredients for the dipping sauce, and wrap the drumsticks individually for delicious beach picnics!

Serves 4-6
30 minutes
425°

sweet barbecue sauce with honey & thyme

This delicious recipe transforms any barbequed meat or poultry into an exquisite meal. It is certainly worth the cooking time and can be made in large batches and frozen.

3 onions, diced

2 garlic cloves, diced

1 bay leaf

6 Tbsps olive oil

4 thyme branches

4 Tbsps cider vinegar

4 Tbsps honey

1 1/2 Tbsps Dijon mustard

1 16-oz can tomatoes, drained & chopped

1 Tbsp tomato paste

1/3 cup Worcester sauce

1/3 cup white wine

Salt and pepper

1 tsp Tabasco sauce

1 In a heavy skillet, heat the oil over a medium heat and add the onions.

2 Cook the onions until soft and golden, then add the tomatoes and vinegar.

3 Bring to a slow boil and add the tomato paste, wine, Worcester sauce, thyme, bay leaf, garlic, honey, and the mustard.

4 Decrease the heat to low and simmer for 25 minutes, adding water if necessary.

5 Add the salt, pepper and Tabasco to taste. Serve with barbequed chicken, spare-ribs, or steak.

the mayan temples

The mythical Atlantis is said to have had a strong influence on the Mayan and Aztec people. Here in Paradise, the vast resort of Atlantis pays tribute to this world of mythology and water with its soaring Mayan temples and eleven-million-gallon gallon aquatic garden holding over 40,000 exotic fish. Visitors can walk amongst the waterfalls, pools and streams and combine a glimpse of an ancient civilization with every manner of vacation activity.

mom's perfect chicken soup with sage & leeks

This is simply the best chicken soup I have ever tasted. I make it in large batches and freeze it for stormy nights or runny noses!

4 chicken thighs

2 onions, chopped

4 Tbsps butter

1 leek, chopped

2 cloves garlic, chopped

1 cup celery, chopped

3 carrots, sliced

3 cups chicken stock

2 bay leaves

2 allspice berries

1 tsp curry

1 tsp sugar

1 bunch fresh thyme

2 Tbsps parsley

1 tsp sage

1 tsp oregano

Salt and pepper

1　In a large pot fry the chicken thighs in butter over a medium heat until brown.

2　Add the onions, leek, and garlic and fry for 2 minutes.

3　Add the celery and fry for 2 more minutes, stirring.

4　Add the carrots, chicken broth, and seasonings with a good amount of salt.

5　Bring to a boil, then turn down the heat to low and simmer, partially covered, for about 1 1/2 hours.

6　Remove the skin and meat of the chicken from the bone and cut into small pieces. Discard the bones and skin and return the meat to the soup.

7　Add a small amount of wide egg-noodles or quick-cooking barley if desired and simmer until soft. Add salt and pepper to taste and serve with warm, crusty bread.

Serves 4
1 1/2 hours

roasted garlic lamb with mustard & parsley crust

This is one the most delicious recipes in the book and is so simple. The flavors of the garlic sauce infuse into the meat as it crusts over during cooking. I make this using a leg or rack of lamb for elegant dinner parties, or just brush the sauce over lamb chops as they fry for a quick dinner for two. It is always spectacular!

8 cloves garlic, chopped

1 cup parsley

1/2 cup Dijon mustard

1/2 cup soy sauce

1 cup olive oil

1 Tbsp sugar

Leg of lamb

Salt to taste

Freshly ground pepper

1 Add the garlic, parsley, mustard, soy sauce, 1 cup of olive oil and sugar to a blender and pulse until the mixture is smooth.

2 Generously spread the garlic mixture over the lamb until it is covered. Let the lamb sit for 1 hour in the refrigerator.

3 Just before cooking, add a little more garlic sauce to the lamb and roast at 350° for about 1 1/2 hours, depending on the size of the lamb.

4 Before serving, heat the remaining sauce in a small pot with 2 tablespoons of olive oil. Carve the lamb and serve drizzled with sauce and mint jelly on the side.

Serves 4-6
1 1/2 hours
350°

the lighthouse

The lighthouse (shown on the next page) on the western tip of Paradise Island was opened on September 1, 1817, to guide ships to safety through Nassau Harbor's rocky entrance. Until its automation in 1958, it was maintained by a keeper who lived in a small house just east of the lighthouse. The remnants of this house are visible today. John Drudge was the longest-serving lighthouse keeper and was famous for staying at his post throughout hurricanes of the worst severity. He was known to have rescued many a sailor during such storms as they were flung from their boats onto the rocks on which the lighthouse stands. Indeed, he even saved his assistant, who was once swept away to sea by a giant wave.

purely pasta

pasta pomodoro

spaghetti alla vongole

spaghetti bolognese

fresh pesto

creamy lasagna

pasta pomodoro with fresh basil & mozzarella cheese

This is my mother's recipe and I have yet to taste a better tomato sauce. You can use canned tomatoes and it is just as good, just a little richer. The sugar in this recipe takes away the acidic taste of the tomatoes. The secret ingredient is the curry-you won't taste it in the final sauce, but it gives a true depth of flavor. Add grilled eggplant cubes to this recipe for a creative alternative.

4 Tbsps olive oil

1 large onion, diced

3 cloves garlic, chopped

5 large tomatoes, or 1 large can tomatoes, drained and coarsely chopped

2 allspice berries

2 bay leaves

1 Tbsp curry powder

1/4 cup fresh basil leaves

1 tsp oregano

3 Tbsp sugar

1/4 tsp hot pepper flakes

Fresh mozzarella cheese

Salt and pepper

1 Fry the chopped onion and garlic in a large skillet over a medium heat until the onion is very soft but not yet brown.

2 Add all but 1/2 of one tomato, the herbs and spices, and the sugar. Stir the sauce well.

3 Bring to a boil and then lower heat, partially cover the skillet, and simmer for 30 minutes stirring occasionally. Add a little water if the sauce gets too dry.

4 Add the reserved tomato and cook for 3 more minutes.

5 Serve with al dente spaghetti and top with olive oil, fresh basil, and mozzarella cheese.

Serves 2

bahamian tomatoes

Tomatoes, in one form or another, are used in almost every typical Bahamian dish. The native tomatoes are large, juicy, and extremely flavorful. They can be found in the fruit and vegetable stalls in Potter's Cay, under the Paradise Island Bridge, or in the colorful stalls on the side of the road.

spaghetti alla vongole with golden garlic & parsley

This dish can be made in almost as much time as it takes to set the table and boil the pasta. I prepare this when we return late from a day of scuba-diving or boating. It is one of our favorites.

3 cloves garlic, chopped

4 Tbsps olive oil

1 can baby clams in water

1 cup chicken stock

1/2 tsp red pepper flakes

1 large tomato, diced

1 Tbsp parsley, chopped

Salt and pepper

1 Fry the garlic and pepper flakes with the olive oil in a large skillet over a medium heat until the garlic is almost golden.

2 Add the chopped tomato and fry for 2 minutes longer.

3 Add the clam water but reserve the clams. Simmer for 5 minutes.

4 Add the chicken stock and leave to simmer for 5-10 minutes or until the liquid is reduced by half.

5 Add the clams and heat for 2 minutes.

6 Cook the spaghetti according to the instructions but remove from the cooking water 1 minute before it is ready. Add the spaghetti to the clam sauce skillet and cook over a high heat for 1 minute, stirring constantly.

7 Sprinkle the spaghetti with parsley to garnish and serve.

Serves 2

spaghetti bolognese with melted parmesan cheese

A rich and hearty dish, this bolognese has yet to be bettered in my opinion! The curry gives it an exotic and yet subtle twist.

4 Tbsps olive oil

1 large onion, diced

1 carrot, chopped

8 mushrooms, quartered

3 cloves garlic, chopped

1/2 lb ground beef

3 Tbsp of red wine

1 12-oz can chopped tomatoes

2 allspice berries

1 Tbsp curry powder

1 tsp basil

2 tsp oregano

3 Tbsp sugar

Salt and pepper

Parmesan and cheddar cheeses

1 Fry the onion, garlic, carrot and mushrooms in olive oil in a large heavy cooking pot until the onion is very soft but not brown.

2 Add the meat and fry until it browns.

3 Add the wine and continue to cook for 1 minute.

4 Add the tomatoes and seasonings and simmer over a low heat, covered, for 1-1 1/2 hours. Add a little water if the sauce becomes too dry.

5 Serve over al dente spaghetti with plenty of grated cheddar and parmesan cheese.

Serves 2

the iron

This monstrosity of metal, the remnants of a blockade-runner from the American Civil War, lies on the western tip of Paradise Island near the lighthouse. This ship had the perilous job of running contraband through the war blockade to a Confederate port. Pursued by the guns of a federal ship, the blockade-runner lost its bearings, mistook the lighthouse light for a guide-light, and ran, full-steam, into the treacherous rocks. It now rests in peace on a lovely stretch of Paradise beach that can only be accessed from the sea.

fresh pesto with parmesan, pepper, & pine nuts

Basil thrives in Nassau and we pick it straight from our garden when we make this dish. Pesto can be stored in an airtight container in the fridge for up to two weeks.

1 cup olive oil

2 cups basil leaves

3 cloves garlic, chopped

1 tsp sugar

1 tsp salt

2 Tbsp parmesan cheese

1 Tbsp water

1/2 cup pine nuts

Ground pepper

8 oz spaghetti

1 Mix all of the pesto ingredients except the nuts in a blender until the pesto makes a smooth paste.

2 Cook the spaghetti according to instructions but remove it from the heat 1 minute before it is ready and drain.

3 Add the pesto to the pasta and stir over a medium heat for 1 minute, adding a little water and olive oil if dry.

4 Serve with a sprinkling of parmesan cheese and lightly fried pine nuts. Add salt and freshly ground pepper freely.

Serves 2-4

creamy lasagna with golden cheddar crust

I use my bolognese sauce from this book to make the lasagna. It can be made and assembled ahead of time and frozen if desired. This is perfect for large, casual parties when you don't want to be confined to the kitchen.

Bolognese sauce made with 1 pound meat and 2 tins tomatoes

8 Tbsp butter

8 Tbsp flour

4 cups whole milk

3 bay leaves

4 allspice berries

1 tsp nutmeg

1/2 cup grated cheddar and parmesan cheeses

Salt and pepper

1 Melt the butter in a heavy saucepan and whisk in the flour.

2 Bring the milk to a gentle boil in a separate pan, remove it from the heat, and add the bay leaves and allspice berries. Let the milk sit for 5 minutes for the flavors to steep.

3 Add the milk to the butter/flour mixture and bring slowly to a boil, stirring constantly with a whisk. Boil gently for 5 minutes and add the nutmeg, salt, and pepper while stirring.

4 Layer the meat sauce, pasta, and white sauce repeatedly in a casserole dish, finishing with the white sauce. Sprinkle the grated cheddar and parmesan cheeses on the top.

5 Bake for 1-1 1/2 hours at 350-375°.

Serves 8
350-375°
1-1 1/2 hours

golfing in paradise

Paradise Island is indeed a golfer's paradise. Redesigned by Tom Weiskopf in 2000 to enhance its seaside tees and greens, the Ocean Club Golf Course was transformed into one of the world's most beautiful courses. This par 72, 18-hole championship course overlooks the Atlantic Ocean and Nassau Harbor with its famous Hole 17 playing entirely along the scenic Snorkeler's Cove. It is certainly worth a visit!

eggs & cheese

tomato & ricotta tart

unbeatable scrambled eggs

twice-baked soufflés

tomato and ricotta tart with arugula and basil leaves

This tart is delicious-its taste and texture are somewhere between a pizza and a quiche. It can be served hot or cold, and is a perfect dish to pack and serve on a beach picnic.

1 package puff pasty

3 ripe tomatoes, sliced

2 cups ricotta cheese

2 eggs, beaten

1/2 cup heavy cream

1/4 cup fresh parmesan, grated

1/2 tsp nutmeg

1/2 tsp salt

1/2 tsp pepper

10 anchovy fillets

1 cup arugula, chopped

1/4 cup fresh basil

1 Salt the tomatoes and leave to drain in a colander.

2 Roll out the puff pastry dough to 1/4-inch thickness and place in a greased baking tray.

3 Mix the ricotta, eggs, cream, parmesan, nutmeg, salt, pepper, and arugula in a large bowl.

4 Spread the mixture over the pastry dough and roll up the sides of the dough to prevent the mixture from spilling over the sides.

5 Arrange the tomatoes decoratively over the tart and sprinkle with anchovies and a few leaves of basil.

6 Bake the tart at 400° for 35-40 minutes, or until the crust is golden and the filling has just set. Serve warm or at room temperature with mixed greens.

Serves 6
40 minutes
400°

the glass sculptures

The four magnificent glass sculptures that decorate the Atlantis casino were commissioned from artist Dale Chihuly, the Washington-born glass sculptor. The Temple of the Sun (shown opposite) has more than 2,300 yellow, orange, and red elements radiating from its core to form a fiery globe. The spectacular Crystal Gate, the Temple of the Moon, and the Atlantis Seaform Chandelier (which displays luminescent jellyfish, anemones, and squid) light the Atlantis ceilings and halls.

unbeatable scrambled eggs with chopped chives

A couple of simple tricks can turn scrambled eggs into a creamy, melting delicacy. They can make an elegant brunch or dinner for two out of the dregs of the fridge. They are worth the small extra effort and you will never return to your old ways!

6 large eggs

2 Tbsps water

1 Tbsp butter

Salt and pepper

Chopped chives

1 Beat the eggs and water in a bowl briefly with a fork until mixed, but do not over-beat. Do not add salt and pepper at this stage since they toughen the eggs.

2 Make a double boiler by filling a large saucepan with boiling water and placing over a medium heat. Melt the butter in a pot placed in the saucepan of boiling water, creating a double boiler effect.

3 Pour the egg mixture into the melted butter and stir the eggs occasionally while cooking very slowly. The eggs should take about 10 minutes to cook.

4 Remove the eggs from the heat just before they are completely set since they will continue to cook as you serve them. These eggs should be slightly runny in consistency. Stir in the salt, pepper, and chopped chives to taste.

5 Wonderful served with smoked salmon or, in leaner times, just toast!

Serves 2

twice-baked soufflés with melted roquefort cheese

These individual soufflés are exquisite. They can be prepared ahead of time so they are perfect for dinner parties. To prepare ahead, complete until the end of step 6, then cool, cover, and chill for up to 24 hours.

2 oz butter

2 oz flour

2 cups milk

10 oz crumbled Roquefort cheese

4 large eggs, separated

1 cup heavy cream

1/4 tsp nutmeg

Salad leaves to garnish

Salt

Ground black pepper

1 Butter six 1-cup ramekin dishes. Line the bases with parchment paper to prevent the soufflés from sticking.

2 Melt the butter in a medium-sized saucepan, whisk in the flour, and mix to a smooth paste. Blend in the milk and bring to a boil, stirring continuously. Remove from the heat.

3 Cool a little, then beat in 6 oz of the cheese and egg yolks. Season well with salt and pepper.

4 Whip the egg whites to firm peaks and fold gently into the cheese mixture. Fill each ramekin 3/4 full with the mixture.

5 Place the ramekins in a roasting tin and add hot water to the tin so that it comes halfway up the side of the ramekins. Bake at 350° for 20 minutes or until the soufflés are firm to the touch.

6 Remove the ramekins from the roasting tin and allow the soufflés to cool for 2 hours. Lightly butter a baking sheet and carefully turn out the soufflés onto the baking sheet.

7 For extra flavor, slice the soufflés in half, horizontally, and place the remaining Roquefort between the top and bottom layers.

8 Add 1 teaspoon of coarse ground pepper and the nutmeg to the cream, and then spoon 2-3 tablespoons on top of each soufflé. Bake at 400° for 20-25 minutes or until golden. Serve immediately, garnished with mixed greens.

Serves 6

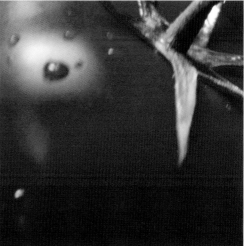

from the garden

bahamian peas 'n rice

creamy potato gratin

honey carrots

eggplant ratatouille

coconut curry

bahamian peas 'n rice with peppers & thyme

Peas 'n rice accompany almost every Bahamian main course. This is a delicious, inexpensive, and very satisfying side dish. For a typical Bahamian meal, I serve it with a twist of lime, steam conch, and coleslaw.

5 slices bacon

1 small onion, diced

1/4 green pepper, diced

1/4 cup tomato paste

1 cup pigeon peas

1 cup rice

2 cups water

1 Tbsp fresh thyme

1 tsp salt

1 Fry the bacon in a skillet until crisp. Remove the bacon and chop into small pieces.

2 Add the onion, green pepper, salt, pepper, and thyme to the bacon fat and fry until the onions become soft and are about to brown.

3 Add the peas, cooked bacon, and uncooked rice and fry for 1 minute, stirring constantly.

4 Stir 2 cups of water or very light chicken broth and the tomato paste into the mixture. Cover and cook until the rice is tender, stirring occasionally.

5 Serve with fish or conch for a true Bahamian dinner.

Serves 2-4

creamy potato gratin with garlic-infused leeks

This is the richest, most flavorful gratin I have ever tasted. The leeks and garlic complement the potatoes perfectly. It is absolutely delicious and makes a perfect side dish to any roasted lamb or meat.

7 cloves garlic, chopped

10 Idaho potatoes

5 large leeks

1/2 cup butter

2 cups heavy cream

1/2 cup parmesan cheese

Lots of salt and pepper!

cook's tip

This dish can be served as a side dish but can also be turned into a delicious and hearty main course by adding a layer of chopped, uncooked pancetta or bacon between the potatoes and leeks.

1 Slice the potatoes and leeks thinly.

2 Butter a heavy casserole dish and cover the dish with a layer of the sliced potatoes.

3 Sprinkle the potatoes liberally with salt, pepper, and chopped garlic. Chop the butter into 1/2-inch squares and sprinkle a generous amount over the potatoes.

4 Cover the potatoes with a layer of sliced leeks followed by another layer of potatoes.

5 Return to step 3 and continue with the layers of potatoes, then salt, pepper and garlic, then butter, then leeks, ending with a layer of potatoes.

6 Pour the heavy cream over the dish and sprinkle parmesan cheese over the top.

7 Bake at 375° for 1-1 1/2 hours or until the potatoes are soft. Cover with foil if the top becomes too brown.

1-1 1/2 hours
Serves 6
375°

honey carrots with tropical rum-butter glaze

Rum is the staple drink of the Bahamas, flowing almost as freely as water! It works well with these carrots, adding depth of flavor and a bit of a kick.

1 pound baby carrots, peeled

1 cup water

3 Tbsp butter

3 Tbsp dark rum

3 Tbsp honey

1 Tbsp dark brown sugar

Salt and pepper

1 Melt the butter in a small pot over a low heat, then carefully pour in the rum.

2 Add the rest of the ingredients to the skillet.

3 Cook the carrots over medium heat, stirring occasionally, for about 10-15 minutes until the carrots are tender and the liquid is reduced to a glaze.

4 Season with a good amount of salt and black pepper.

Serves 4

the dune restaurant

The Dune Restaurant, located on the sandy precipice of the Ocean Club, looks out over the turquoise waters of Cabbage Beach and is certainly one of the Caribbean's best restaurants. The renowned New York chef Jean-George Vongerichten teamed up with French designer Christian Liaigre to create this exquisite restaurant. Diners can enjoy exotic cuisine with a Bahamian accent while enjoying the breathtaking view.

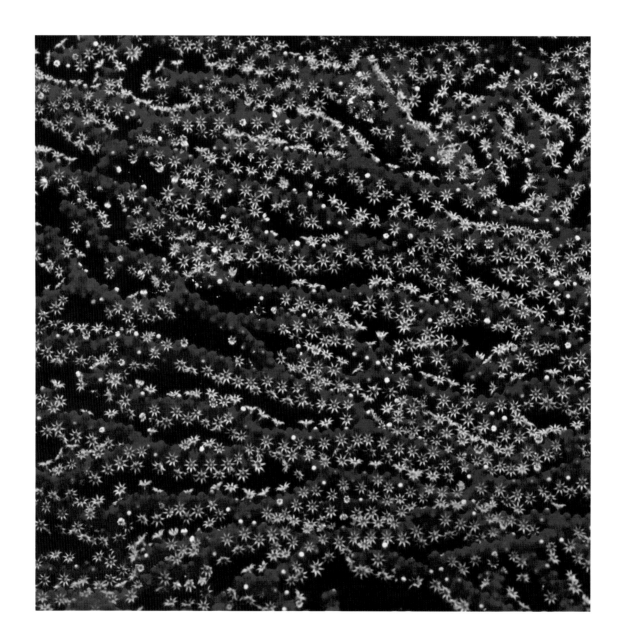

eggplant ratatouille with roasted garlic & thyme

Tomatoes, peppers, and thyme are grown in abundance in the Bahamas and are delicious here. This dish is wonderfully fresh and flavorful. I usually make it in large batches and serve it cold for lunch or warm with rice for a light dinner.

1 medium eggplant

1 green pepper

1 zucchini

5 fresh tomatoes

1 onion

3 cloves garlic, chopped

1/3 cup olive oil

6 sprigs fresh thyme

2 Tbsps fresh basil

1 bay leaf

1 Slice and cube the eggplant. Shake salt generously over the cubes and leave them in a colander for an hour to drain. Dry with paper towels.

2 Coarsely chop the other vegetables.

3 Fry the eggplant cubes for 1 minute in the olive oil and remove.

4 Fry the green pepper, onion, and garlic in the oil for 1 minute. Add the eggplant, zucchini, chopped tomatoes, and herbs and fry, stirring, for 2 minutes.

5 Place all of the vegetable in a baking dish, sprinkle with olive oil, and bake uncovered for 40 minutes at 375°. Serve hot accompanied by rice or cold as a side dish.

Serves 2-4
40 minutes
375°

coconut curry with lemongrass & ginger essence

This is a wonderful one-dish dinner. You can make the recipe as is or you can add more chicken broth to make a delicious soup.

1 Tbsp fresh ginger, grated

3 cloves garlic, chopped

2 sticks lemongrass

3 Tbsps sesame oil

1 cup mushrooms, chopped

1 cup broccoli heads

1 cup red peppers, sliced

2 Tbsps Thai green curry paste

1 can coconut milk

1 cup chicken broth

2 Tbsp soy sauce

1/3 cup mirin or sherry

5-6 skinned chicken fillets or 1 cup shrimp, peeled

Cilantro & crushed peanuts for garnish

1 Heat the wok over a high heat and add the oil, ginger, lemongrass, and garlic. Stir-fry for 1 minute.

2 If using chicken fillets, add these and fry for 4 minutes to brown but do not cook through. Remove the chicken. If using shrimp, do not cook them at this point.

3 Add the vegetables and stir-fry for 4 minutes.

4 Add the curry paste and cook for 1 minute.

5 Add the coconut milk, chicken broth, soy sauce, mirin or sherry and browned chicken breasts and simmer for 6 minutes, until the sauce is reduced. If you are using shrimp, add them during the last minute of cooking.

6 Serve in bowls with cilantro and crushed peanuts. Serve basmati or jasmine rice towers on the side.

Serves 2

cook's tip

You can substitute 2 Tbsp red curry powder and 2 Tbsp smooth peanut butter for the green curry paste to make a delicious red-curry version of this dish.

sweet endings

pecan puffs

sweet potato pie

heirloom apple cake

piled-high pavlova

burnt orange tart

tarte tatin

heavenly peach cake

lemon meringue pie

walnutrum cake

banana mini soufflés

pecan puffs with sweet strawberry filling

This is an old American recipe that my mother often made. These cookies melt on the tongue-they are heavenly!

1/2 cup of butter, softened

2 Tbsp sugar

1 tsp vanilla

1 cup of pecans, finely ground

1 cup flour

1/2 cup strawberry jam

flamingos

The flamingo is the Bahamian national bird and can be found in vast colonies in Great Inagua, where they feast on brine shrimp, thus giving them their brilliant pink color.

1 With a hand-mixer, beat the butter until smooth.

2 Add the sugar and vanilla and beat briefly.

3 Mix in the ground pecans and flour by hand.

4 Scoop up about a tablespoon of the dough at a time and roll the dough into small balls between your palms.

5 Place the balls on a greased baking sheet.

6 If you want to fill with jam after cooking, put a dent in each cookie with your finger.

7 Bake the cookies at 325° for 25 minutes or until they are very light golden.

8 Allow to cool and fill each with a teaspoon of strawberry compote or jam.

25 minutes
325°

sweet potato pie & vanilla-scented whipped cream

This pie is incredibly versatile. Canned pumpkin can be substituted for sweet potatoes and almost any combination of milk/cream and sugar can be used-the exact quantities need not be measured perfectly. Just dip a finger in the mixture before it goes in the oven, and if it tastes good it will come out fine!

9-inch pie crust

4-5 large sweet potatoes

2 large eggs

1 cup milk

1 cup heavy cream

1 cup light brown sugar

1 tsp cinnamon

1/4 tsp cloves

1/2 tsp nutmeg

1 tsp vanilla

1 Preheat the oven to 350° and bake the sweet potatoes for 1 hour or until soft. (Can be done a day ahead.)

2 Bake the pie crust in a pie dish at 350° for 10 minutes.

3 Mix the cooked, peeled sweet potatoes with the rest of the ingredients and beat with a hand-mixer for 3 minutes.

4 Pour the mixture into the warm pie shell. Bake for 1 hour or until the filling is just set.

5 Serve the pie cold with vanilla whipped cream made with 2 cups whipping cream, 1/3 cup sugar, and 1/2 teaspoons of vanilla essence.

Serves 6-8
1 hour
350°

heirloom apple cake with walnuts and raisins

This recipe was passed down from my great-grandmother and is absolutely delicious. It is best when cooled and left to sit for at least a few hours before serving to let the cake become moist and the flavors deepen. You can use either a springform pan or a large pie dish to make this tasty treat.

1/2 tsp salt

3/4 tsp baking soda

1 tsp cinnamon

1/4 tsp cloves

3/4 tsp nutmeg

1/2 cup vegetable oil

2 eggs

1 tsp vanilla

2 cups apples, chopped into roughly 1/2-inch squares

1/2 cup walnuts

1/2 cup raisins

1 cup sugar

1 cup flour

1 In a bowl mix the salt, baking soda, cinnamon, cloves, and nutmeg.

2 Add the oil, eggs, and vanilla and whisk together with a hand whisk until well mixed.

3 Mix in the apples, nuts, sugar, and raisins.

4 Mix in the flour, a little at a time.

5 Pour the mixture into a greased springform baking pan or deep pie dish.

6 Bake at 350° for 45 minutes to an hour or until a toothpick inserted in the center of the cake comes out clean.

Serves 6
350°
1 hour

cook's tip

For a more tropical version of this cake, substitute chopped, ripe bananas for the apples and add 3/4 cup chocolate chips to the batter.

piled-high pavlova with cream and berry filling

This is a wonderful summer dessert. The meringue is crispy on the outside and chewy within. It complements the fruit perfectly .

4 egg whites

1 tsp cornstarch

1 tsp vinegar

1 tsp vanilla

6 oz sugar

2 cups whipping cream

1/4 cup sugar for cream

2 cups fresh berries

cook's tip

For a deliciously tangy, tropical taste, substitute passionfruit pulp for the berries.

1 Beat the egg whites with an electric beater until the whites form soft peaks.

2 Add the sugar, a little at a time.

3 Add the cornstarch, vinegar, and vanilla and beat thoroughly until the mixture has a glossy shine (about 7 minutes).

4 Line a baking sheet with parchment paper and grease lightly.

5 Pile the stiff egg whites onto the baking sheet, arranging decoratively with a spatula. Leave a dent in the center for the fruit.

6 Bake for 1 1/2 hours at 200° and then turn off the oven and let the meringue sit for 1 more hour (cover with foil lightly if it begins to brown).

7 When cooled, spoon whipped cream, made from 2 cups whipping cream with 1/4 cup sugar, into the center of the meringue.

8 Spoon fresh berries on top of the cream and serve.

Serves 4-6
1 hour
200°

burnt orange tart with crispy caramel crust

This tart is a Bahamian slant on the traditional french lemon tart. Bahamian oranges are among the sweetest that can be found. This tart is easy to make and wonderfully delicate. The trick is to broil the powdered sugar coating the pie at the end, which forms a light caramel crust much like that of a creme brulée.

1 pie crust pastry

5 large eggs

1 cup sugar

1 cup fresh orange juice

2 Tbsp fresh lemon juice

2 tsp grated orange rind

3/4 cup whipping cream

3 Tbsp powdered sugar

1 Mix the eggs, sugar, juice, rind, and cream with a hand-mixer.

2 Pour into a partially baked crust and bake at 325° for about 40 minutes or until filling is set.

3 Refrigerate until cold, then cover the top of the crust with strips of foil while leaving the filling exposed.

4 Sprinkle the tart with the powdered sugar and place it under the broiler until the sugar turns golden brown and melts.

5 Cool the tart and serve at room temperature with fresh berries.

Serves 6
40 minutes
325°

tarte tatin with caramelized pecans & creme fraiche

This tarte tatin is a staple in our family-it makes for a spectacular finale at dinner parties or a comforting dessert after a dinner for two. Cold leftovers make a perfect summer breakfast.

1 package puff pastry

6 Tbsp butter

2/3 cup sugar

1 tsp grated lemon zest

2 1/2 lbs Granny Smith apples cored and sliced into quarters

1/2 cup pecans (optional)

1 cup creme fraiche

1 Melt the butter in a skillet over a medium flame, then gradually add the sugar. Stir until it begins to bubble and dissolve (~2 minutes).

2 Add the lemon zest and pecans (optional) and stir.

3 Remove the pan from the heat and add the apples, arranging decoratively.

4 Cover and cook over a medium heat for 5 minutes, then remove from the heat.

5 Roll out the pastry dough and carefully lay it over the apples in the skillet, tucking the sides in around the apples.

6 Place the skillet in the oven and bake at 375° for 40 minutes. Turn out after 1 minute and serve with creme fraiche sweetened to taste.

Serves 6
40 minutes
375°

heavenly peach cake with crunchy streusel topping

This Caribbean version of the traditional coffee cake uses ripe peaches instead of brown sugar to give moisture and flavor. Canned peaches work wonderfully if peaches are not in season.

Cake:
2/3 cup sugar

4 oz butter

1 tsp vanilla

2 large eggs

1 cup cake flour

3/4 tsp baking powder

1/2 tsp salt

8 ripe peaches, peeled and quartered, or 2 cans sliced peaches, drained

Streusel:
1 cup flour

3/4 cup brown sugar

6 Tbsp butter

1 tsp cinnamon

1 Cream the butter, sugar, and vanilla using an electric beater until fluffy.

2 Add the eggs and dry ingredients and beat until mixed.

3 Pour the batter into a buttered 9-inch cake tin.

4 Arrange the peach slices over the batter.

5 Make the topping by rubbing the streusel ingredients together with your hands.

6 Spread the streusel topping over the cake.

7 Bake at 350° for 50 minutes to 1 hour, or until a toothpick inserted in the cake comes out clean.

Serves 6
1 hour
350°

fluffy lemon meringue pie with zesty lemon crust

Crust:

1 1/4 cup all purpose flour

2 Tbsp sugar

1 tsp grated lemon rind

6 Tbsp cold butter

3 Tbsp ice water

Filling:

1 1/2 cups water

1 cup sugar

1/2 cup lemon juice

5 egg yolks

4 Tbsp cornstarch

3 Tbsp grated lemon peel

3 Tbsp butter

Meringue:

7 large egg whites

1/2 tsp baking soda

1 1/2 cups powdered sugar

1 Pulse the flour, sugar, and lemon rind together quickly in a food processor. Cut the butter into small squares and add to the mixture. Pulse until just mixed.

2 Add the water, a teaspoon at a time, and mix. Pat the dough together, wrap in plastic wrap, and refrigerate for at least 1 hour.

3 Roll out the dough and line a pie dish. Pierce with a fork, then cover closely with foil. Bake at 400° for 15 minutes, then uncover and bake 10 more minutes.

4 Whisk together the first 6 filling ingredients and stir over a medium heat for 10 minutes.

5 Remove the mixture from the heat and stir in the butter.

6 Beat the egg whites until fairly stiff and add the baking soda.

7 Beat in the sugar a little at a time. Beat at high speed for 7 minutes until the whites are stiff and glossy.

8 Assemble the pie by pouring the lemon-egg mixture into the crust first, then covering it completely with the beaten egg whites.

9 Bake the pie at 300° for 1 hour, covering with foil if it becomes too brown. Serve with mixed berries.

Serves 6

walnut rum cake with sugared-rum glaze

This quintessential Bahamian dessert is found at almost every Bahamian restaurant and bakery. Every rum cake is a little different. This version is my favorite and has the advantage of using a pre-prepared cake mix!

Cake:
1 cup chopped pecans or walnuts

1 18 1/2-oz. pkg. yellow cake mix

1 3 3/4-oz. pkg. Jell-O vanilla instant pudding

4 eggs

1/2 cup cold water

1/2 cup vegetable oil

1/2 cup Bacardi dark rum (80 proof)

Glaze:
8 oz butter

1/4 cup water

1 cup granulated sugar

1/3 cup Bacardi dark rum

1 Preheat oven to 325°. Grease and flour a bundt pan.

2 Sprinkle nuts over the bottom of the pan. Mix all of the cake ingredients together and beat for 2 minutes.

3 Pour the batter over the nuts, bake for 1 hour, then cool.

4 Prepare the glaze by melting the butter in a sauce pan and stirring in the water and sugar. Boil for 5 minutes, stirring constantly, then remove from the heat and stir in rum.

5 Prick holes in the cake with a knife and pour the glaze over the cake, allowing it to absorb the glaze.

6 Allow the cake to sit for 5 minutes, then invert it onto a serving plate. Serve with vanilla ice cream.

Serves 6
1 hour
325°

the ocean club spa

The experience at the Ocean Club Spa is one of ultimate indulgence. Each guest is attended to in his own private villa, a secluded sanctuary in which he receives spa treatments, bathes in petal-strewn baths, and is served herbal teas and fresh fruit. The experience is magnificent!

banana mini soufflés with melted chocolate chunks

Banana Base:

2 oz butter

1/3 cup brown sugar

1/4 cup sugar

6 very ripe bananas chopped into 1/2-inch pieces

2 Tbsps dark rum

2 Tbsps lemon juice

Soufflé:

2 tablespoons butter, softened

1/3 cup sugar, for dusting

12 egg whites

4 ounces powdered sugar

2 ounces bittersweet chocolate chips

1. Heat the butter in a medium saucepan over a high heat until golden brown.

2. Add the sugar and continue to cook, stirring constantly, for 4-5 minutes until golden.

3. Stir in the bananas and cook for 2 minutes more, then remove from heat and stir in the rum and lemon juice.

4. Transfer the mixture to a food processor and pulse until smooth. Allow the mixture to cool.

5. Butter the insides of 6 1-cup ramekins and dust with sugar.

6. Beat the egg whites to soft peaks, then add the sugar slowly, continuing to whip to medium-stiff peaks.

7. With a large rubber spatula, fold 1/2 of the meringue into the banana base. Add the chocolate chips and fold into the remaining 1/2 of the meringue.

8. Fill each ramekin with the soufflé mixture and bake the soufflés for 12 minutes at 375°. Serve immediately dusted with powdered sugar and with a side of vanilla ice cream.

Serves 6
15 minutes
375°